Beautiful Winter
For Kids

Nature Books for Kids
By K. Bennett
Mendon Cottage Books

JD-Biz Publishing

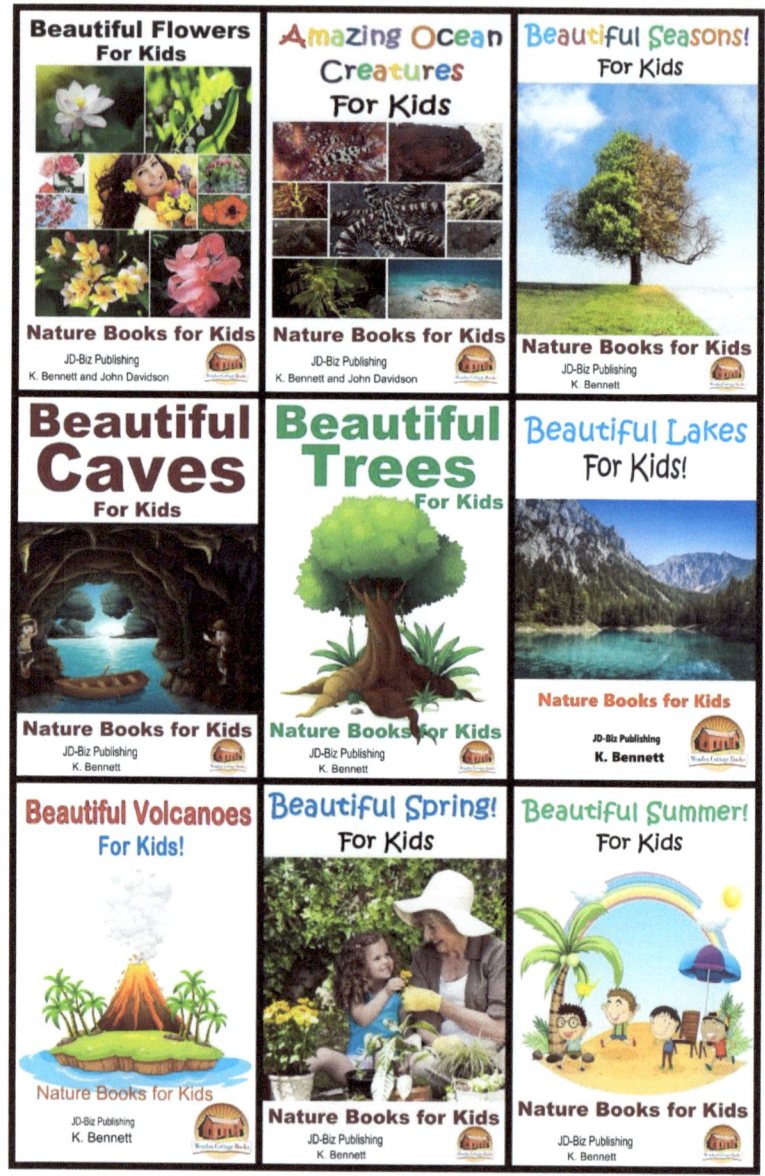

Table of Contents

Introduction

Winter: Winter is a beautiful season when the days are short and the nights are long and cold.

During wintertime, you will find the lowest temperatures on planet earth, and snow starts to fall from the sky!

Lots of really cold things happen during winter like blizzards, sleet, hail, and freezing rain! Brrrrrrrr…Even plant life is affected during the cold months.

Trees and plants stop growing, and animals like to hibernate and stay out of the cold. Other creatures migrate to warmer places and wait until winter goes away. Do you remember what kind of animals migrate to escape the winter cold?

In our book *Beautiful Autumn for Kids*, we talked a little about it.

What is migration:

This word basically means when animals move from one place to another and then back again. Think of it like a plane ticket from Miami to New York and then back to Miami again!

These animals use many different ways to escape the cold. Some use the sun, others use the stars and many use the earth's magnetic field.

Here is a list of some creatures that leave for warmer places:

-Snow geese

-Monarch butterflies

-Swallows

-Rufous hummingbirds

-Rattle snakes

-Gopher snakes

-Humpback whales

-Dolphins

-Elk

-Robins

-Some insects

-Wild caribou and many more!

What about humans? Do we migrate from one place to another?
Think about it and share your findings with others!

Why does it get so cold in winter?

Let's talk about the angle of the earth and why we have four seasons.
The reason why we have these changes is because of the earth's tilt
towards the sun.

Do you remember how many degrees the earth is tilted? Choose a
number…

1- $14.76°$ (Fourteen point seventy-six degrees)

2- $20.22°$ (Twenty point twenty-two degrees.)

3- $23.45°$ (Twenty-three point forty-five degrees.)

If you chose number 3… you are correct!

This is what gives the earth the beautiful seasons during the year like
winter. If you want to know what this means imagine this…

Think of yourself as leaning forward (without holding on to anything) or to the side without falling over! That's tilting! This is what the earth does.

This is why planet earth has such amazing seasons! If the earth did not tilt at this angle, we would have the same season every single day of the year! Does that sound a little boring? I think so!

It is important to remember that some places in the world do not have four different seasons, but only two: wet and dry! It is also called dry season and rainy season. Can you find those places on a map? Get someone to help you look!

How are things different in winter?

During this special season, the sun hits the earth at a different angle or a different way. *Planet-sciecne.com* says two things change: First, "the Northern Hemisphere is tilted away from the sun." And second, "the sun is lower the sky during winter, which changes the angle of the light hitting us and how much heat energy we get from it." This is why it gets so cold!

Winter is a great time for families to get together and share wonderful memories. And this book on Beautiful Winter will remind you just how much fun winter can be! I hope you enjoy learning more about this amazing part of earth's natural wonders.

Chapter 1: Winter Weather

Lots of different things happen during wintertime. Can you think of some things that change? In the beginning, we talked about blizzards, sleet, hail, and freezing rain. Do you know what these words mean?

Let's find out!

Blizzards: Our daily weather is caused by lots of different things happening at the same time.

A blizzard is a very bad snow storm when two pressures run into each other. One is low and one is high. This is called a: low pressure system and a high pressure system. Have you ever heard about this before?

Weatherwizkids.com has a neat way to explain what these terms mean.

High pressure system:

This type of system is represented by a big blue… **H**

Low pressure system:

The low pressure system is represented by a big red… **L**

A high pressure system has cool, dry air whirling around. It brings really nice weather with light wind and beautiful sunny skies! This type of wind spins clockwise.

A low pressure system has warm air with lots of moisture. It brings stormy weather and strong winds with little sunlight. This type of wind spins counterclockwise.

When both of these pressure systems touch each other, can you guess what happens? Yes, a blizzard starts!

The temperatures drop very low and the wind starts to spin around with lots of snow. This type of weather is dangerous, so it is better to stay inside until the blizzard is over.

You should also have extra batteries for your radio or flashlight. Candles, water, food and a charged cell phone are good choices too!

Sleet: This type of weather is a mix between rain and snow. Did you know some raindrops freeze on the way down? This is called ice pellets.

Sleet does not happen all the time. To get this type of weather, we need two different weather patterns to mix together. Near the ground, we need to have a space of air that is below freezing. Above this space of air, we need to have a space of warmer air.

When the snow falls from the sky and hits the space with warm air, it melts into raindrops. Sometimes it does not melt all the way, but it gets soft enough to turn into cold water.

The snow then falls through the space of air that is below freezing and it re-freezes again!

So instead of beautiful snowflakes, you get re-frozen water that turns into ice pellets…then it hits the ground. This might sound dangerous, but it is not that bad. Sleet is usually light and bounces when it hits the ground!

Did you understand how it works? Good job! If you still need more information, ask your parent or a guardian to help you research online!

Hail: This weather pattern also forms ice pellets, but it is different from sleet. One reason is because it forms in clouds and not near the ground. Usually, hail falls during thunderstorms and can fall even in the spring and summer!

Freezing rain: This happens when raindrops fall through a cold space of air close to the ground. But the drops do not freeze until they touch something!

For example, when the liquid water touches the branches of a tree, the rain freezes immediately and that's called freezing rain!

FUN WINTER FACTS FOR KIDS:

Many animals hibernate during the wintertime. This just means they like to sleep when it's cold and wake up when it gets warm again.

Usually, this happens in spring and summer. Some creatures have really cool ways of staying alive during the winter days. Let's talk about three of them!

Wood frogs: These little creatures like to hibernate in logs, under rocks and under leaves or in burrows. But guess what? Wood frogs stop breathing when they hibernate and they get little bits of ice inside their blood! You might think the frog is dead, but when spring starts, these little creatures brush off the cold, defrost and wake back up again!

What do you think about that?

Ground squirrels: These amazing creatures have lots of room in their tunnels to spend the cold days. Did you know they have rooms for storing food, sleeping and even to use the bathroom? Isn't that a very smart squirrel?

Hamsters: These lovely creatures do a light hibernation from time to time, which means they can wake up pretty easily. But hamsters do not like to wake up from hibernation. Why? Because it can scare them to death! They can have a heart attack or fall over dead, so you need to be careful. It is better to leave them alone and let them wake up when they are ready.

Many other creatures have amazing hibernation skills. Would you like to continue learning more? Log on to the Conservation Institute and find 10 animals that hibernate.

Happy learning!

(Source: *http://www.conservationinstitute.org/10-animals-that-hibernate/*)

Chapter 2: Why we love a safe winter

There are lots of reasons why winter is the best season! And here are five quick reasons:

Reason # 1: A nice hot chocolate drink. If you are very cold, don't you think a nice warm drink is a good choice? Or would you prefer something ice cold…brrrrrrrr! Something warm is much better.

Reason # 2: Great food like bread, jams, and cookies. What's your favorite wintertime cookie? Yum! Yum!

Reason # 3: Snuggling. Isn't it great to snuggle with friends and family when it's very cold outside?

Reason # 4: No bugs to bite you. It's too cold outside for them to fly around!

Reason # 5: Fun wintertime activities like building a snowman with a big orange nose! What else do you like to do during winter?

This season can be lots and lots of fun, but there are some important things to remember. Let's learn how to enjoy the season in a safe way.

Be safe during wintertime!

Here are some good tips to think about. Are you ready?

-Wear good, warm clothing and good shoes.

- If there is a storm, DO NOT go outside. Wait until the storm passes and ask your parent's or a guardian's permission to play outdoors.

-Don't stick your tongue to very cold things like metal bars or doors. I know your friends may have fun doing it, but please do NOT try things like that. You could get hurt and your parents will NOT be happy!

-Do not play near snowplows or snow blowers. These machines remove snow, but they can really hurt you. Please be careful around this type of equipment!

-Make sure your clothing and shoes or boots are warm and dry at all times. If it gets wet, go inside right away and change.

-Don't forget to wear a hat. You need to protect your head too!

-If you use a sled or race down the side of a hill, use a helmet. Remember to protect your head!

-Don't make tunnels or forts in the snow. Why? Because it could cave in and you can get really hurt! Please be safe at all times.

-Don't throw snowballs at others. Yes, I know it sounds like a lot of fun, but you could hurt someone and someone might hurt you. Build a snowman, snowwoman, or snow dog instead!

These tips are to help you be safe. Don't forget to share your tips with friends and family so they can be safe too!

(Source: http://www.ncbi.nlm.nih.gov/)

FUN WINTER EXPERIMENT!

This is a fun winter experiment adapted from **weatherwizkids. com** Have fun trying this at home and get your friends to try it too!

You will only need two things:

1-Black paper or black material (fabric)
2-Magnifying glass

This is what you need to do:

-Put your black paper or black material in the freezer for a few hours. Then take it out of the freezer and put it outside when the snow is falling from the sky.

-Wait until some flakes land on the paper or material.

-Carefully gather the paper or material and use a magnifying glass to see what interesting shapes you can find.

Did you know no two snowflakes are the same? What kind of shapes do you like the most? Share your findings with your friends, family or teacher!

FUN FACTS FOR KIDS:

There are twelve months in a calendar year. Can you guess which months are: Spring, Summer, Autumn and Winter?

Spring: March, April, and May

Summer: June, July, and August

Autumn: September, October and November (This season is also called: Fall)

Winter: December, January, and February.

Which season do you like best? Think about your reasons, write them down or share with others!

Do you want to make a snowman?

There are lots of fun things you might like to try during this season. Is building a snowman one of them? Here is great idea from ***WikiHow.com*** on how to make a snowman.

These are the supplies you will need for your project:

-Snow and lots of it!
-Warm clothing (gloves, good snow shoes, a hat, a scarf)
-Lots of space to build the snowman

Can you think of anything else to add to this list? Your snowman will need some supplies too! Here is another list to help you.

-Use buttons, rocks, coal or whatever other objects you like for the eyes, mouth and buttons. Use a carrot for the nose and you will need a hat, scarf and gloves for the snowman too!

Now that your supplies are ready, let's start to build.

1. Find a good place to put your snowman. Try to do it on a flat place so it can stand up straight!

2. The snow needs to be thick… not light and fluffy. Try to roll a ball and see if it holds together. If it doesn't hold, it is not good for a snowman!

3. When the snow is ready, roll some of it to make a ball. When you have a small ball, place it on the ground and start to roll it through nice, thick snow. When you roll the ball, it will gather more and more snow. Keep rolling until it gets big enough for you. This will be the bottom part of the snowman.

4. Roll some more snow and make another ball. Try to make it smaller than the first ball. This will be the middle part of the snowman.

5. Roll one more ball to make the head! It should be smaller than the middle ball.

6. When your snowman is ready, pack some snow between the space around the balls to make sure your snowman stands up straight!

7. Add the eyes, the nose, the mouth, the buttons, the hat and the scarf.

8. Add some sticks for the arms and put the gloves on them. If you don't like the gloves, just leave the sticks.

9. Your snowman is ready! Take a nice picture and show your friends and family. Did you do a good job? I am sure you did!

Chapter 3: Winter Facts

I hope you have enjoyed this book on Beautiful Winter! Here are just a few more neat facts you may like to learn about.

- Snowflakes are made up of different ice crystals. Can you guess how many ice crystals make up one snowflake?

1- 50?

2- 100?

3- 200?

Which number did you choose? If you chose number 3 you are correct!! There are around 200 ice crystals in one snowflake.

- Do you know how much fresh water comes from snow and ice?

1- 20%

2- 80%

3- 40%

The correct answer is number 2. Around 80% of the fresh water supply on planet earth comes from snow and ice!

-Would you like to try some watermelon snow? Does it sound tasty? If you ate it, you might not like it very much. Watermelon snow is full of algae, which makes the snow a reddish color. That's why it's called watermelon snow!

-Snow helps the planet to stay cool. When the light from the sun hits the earth, they bounce off the snow and right back into space!

-Snow is not always white. If there is too much pollution it can change the color of the snow. It might look a little gray or a dull white.

-In Maine, they built one of the biggest snowmen ever! He was 122 feet tall! How tall are you?

- In Silver Lake Colorado during 1921, seventy-six inches of snow fell in one day! That is six feet and four inches of snow, that's taller than most adults. What a lot of snow!

- Have you ever heard of thunder snow? This happens when snow falls during a lightning and thunder storm!

-What is one of the biggest activities people like to do in wintertime? Did you guess build a snowman? Great job!

(Source: http://www.kidsplayandcreate.com/what-is-snow-made-of-snowflake-facts-for-kids/)

Vocabulary:

During the winter season, you will hear many different words that people use. Words like:

-Balaclava	-Duvet	-Fruitcake
-Anorak	-Down coat	-Flannel
-Artic	-Frostbitten	-Insulation
-Firewood	-Curling	-Pinecone
-Flurries	-Comforting	-Parka
-Blustery	-Dreary	-Solstice
-Hibernate	-Cocoon	-Wind chill factor
-Chimney	-Sugarplum	-Toboggan
-Hailstone	-Ice hockey	-Woolens

Do you know what any of these words mean? If you are not sure, ask your parent or a guardian's permission to search for the definition. I hope you learn something new! (*www.dictionary.com*)

Conclusion:

In conclusion: Winter is very special season and a time for us to make wonderful memories. Here are a few more ideas to help you learn more!

More Ideas!

Why don't you do some research to learn more about snowflakes? They are called snow crystals and have six sides. Do you know how many types of snow crystals fall from the sky? Can you guess? Here are three of them I would like to share with you.

-Star. (This amazing crystal are some of the most common types of snowflakes. They are very beautiful and fall when the temperature reaches -15 degrees Celsius!)

-Dendrites. (These snow crystals have three dimensional shapes! They also have branches and arms and fall when the temperate gets very cold. Can you guess how cold? -20 to -25 degrees Celsius!)

-Columns. (These types of crystals form when the air is dry. They are usually smaller than stars and dendrites but a little thicker. They can fall when the temperature gets to -15 to - 25 degrees Celsius!)

Something else to think of!

Think of show and tell at school or another school project. Can you talk about winter activities and share with your teacher and classmates? Maybe you can tell them why you like it so much and what makes it different from other seasons!

Just one more!

When does the December solstice happen? Do you know what this means? Become a science journalist and start digging!

The December solstice starts on December 21st. Did you know it is called the Winter Solstice in the Northern Hemisphere, but in the Southern Hemisphere it is called the Summer solstice?

The Winter Solstice is the shortest day of the year, but the Summer solstice is the longest day of the year. How can it be so different and why?

You may choose to make this subject a science project or an experiment. If you do, don't forget the steps you need to do to make it a good science project.

Steps:

1 – You need to ask a **question** to be answered by observation or experimentation. Make it a very interesting question so your classmates and teachers will be excited to learn the answer!

2 – The next step is to state a **Hypothesis**. This is a big word but Sciencekidsathome.com explains it like this*: It is a tentative explanation for an observation, phenomenon, or scientific problem that can be tested by further investigation.*

So your hypothesis is what you think the results of your project will be when your research is all done!

3 – Next thing to think about is: **Procedure.** This is very important. Procedure will help you to find the answer to your question and prove what you are trying to say.

4 – **Results**. You will need to show your results and all of the information you collected for your project.

5 – **Conclusion**. Finish up with what you learned and then answer the question you had in Step 1. If you are unable to answer the question, this is also a great place to put the reasons why the question cannot be answered.

(Source: *www.randroades.wcpss.net*)

I know you will have fun learning about nature and all its wonders! And there are lots more you can still learn if you just take the time to open your eyes and "see" the world around you.

If you don't like the ideas in this book, put on your thinking cap and come up with your own conclusions! I am sure you will do an amazing job!

We hope you have enjoyed this book on Beautiful Winter and always remember…

"Educating the mind without educating the heart is no education at all." - *Aristotle*

Happy Learning!

Author Bio

K. Bennett loves to write for both children and adults. Many different subjects are interesting to research, but writing for children is special to her heart.

Her favorite pastimes include reading, traveling and discovering new things. Each of these activities helps to fuel her imagination and acts like a blank canvas waiting for more stories.

She is intrigued with fantasy elements like hidden worlds and faraway lands. And basically anything that gets her imagination soaring to new heights!

Her writing credits include children books online, short stories for online magazines, and novellas listed at Amazon.com

Check out some of the other JD-Biz Publishing books

Our books are available at

1. Amazon.com

2. Barnes and Noble

3. Itunes

4. Kobo

5. Smashwords

6. Google Play Books

Download Free Books!
http://MendonCottageBooks.com

Publisher

JD-Biz Corp

P O Box 374

Mendon, Utah 84325

http://www.jd-biz.com/

www.ingramcontent.com/pod-product-compliance
Lightning Source LLC
Chambersburg PA
CBHW050850290526
45792CB00002B/596